Lungs

poems by

Chris Bullard

Finishing Line Press
Georgetown, Kentucky

Lungs

Copyright © 2025 by Chris Bullard
ISBN 979-8-88838-946-1 First Edition
All rights reserved under International and Pan-American Copyright Conventions. No part of this book may be reproduced in any manner whatsoever without written permission from the publisher, except in the case of brief quotations embodied in critical articles and reviews.

ACKNOWLEDGMENTS

Bear Review: "Various Absences"
BlazeVox: "Where to Put Death"
Constellations: "Close Call"
Feral: "In Lieu of Flowers"
Hole in the Head Review: "Day of the Dead;" "Lungs"
Jersey Devil Press: "La Poesie Me Volera Ma Mort"
Star*82: "The Future"
VERDANT Journal: "Unsolved Mysteries"
Nailpolish Stories: "Barely There"
New English Review: "Guilty" "Obit"
North of Oxford: "Foster's Rule"

Publisher: Leah Huete de Maines
Editor: Christen Kincaid
Cover Art: Janice K. Bullard
Author Photo: Janice K. Bullard
Cover Design: Elizabeth Maines McCleavy

Order online: www.finishinglinepress.com
also available on amazon.com

Author inquiries and mail orders:
Finishing Line Press
PO Box 1626
Georgetown, Kentucky 40324
USA

Contents

Guilt 1

Unsolved Mysteries 2

Day of the Dead 3

Various Absences 4

Close Call 5

Obit 6

The Future 7

Foster's Rule 8

Where to Put Death 9

Clearing Things Out 10

Double-zero 11

Sadly 12

Arrangement 13

Barely There 14

In Lieu of Flowers 15

La Poesie Me Volera Ma Mort 17

Lungs 18

To Jan

"*A million miles azure pure—the eye reaches beyond what ruined our lives.*"
Li Po, Translated by David Hinton

Guilt

Leaky as a cracked cement
cistern, my mind retains
only a residue of facts,
circling like fallen leaves
around the miry bottom
of the tank, not enough
in memory's fountain
for a thirsty dog to lap.

History I've dammed
behind excuses steams away,
wisps from a kettle held
above the gas flame's hiss,
evaporating heavenward,
like a summer rain reversed.
The angel's share departs,
bearing with it my misdeeds.

Am I thus forgiven?
I can't be blamed for what
I don't possess. My sins
have names that I've forgotten,
like classmates in old albums,
their weight as indeterminate
as the sum of sleeping pills
I've taken from the bottle.

Unsolved Mysteries

Breath stops; bones go on forever
though pitched into coal black rivers

or hidden under stones, the hard
parts of life refuse to be ignored,

as they're stumbled over by hunters,
uncovered by children playing

hide and go seek, remains of murders
and massacres consigned to the amnesia

of undergrowth, emerging like relentless
spring blooms edging to the surface,

frost tossed, rain soaked, connective
tissue that survives to give witness

to what humans do to each other,
overturning our faith in the ground

we trust to walk over like new snow
covering secrets up so beautifully.

Day of the Dead
Calaveras Literarias

I'd buried my past selves in desert graves
where the authorities wouldn't look.
Now, they've returned, dressed in my clothes,
masked with my likeness,
assuming a seat at the table.

Don't they know how I've celebrated
the years of their absence?
I won't share their bitter jokes.
I won't scar the altar with their empty bottles.
I'm telling them to go.

I wish them into that outer world
beyond my caring. The soul I clawed back
from a sand filled skull, I offer only to you,
who breathed life into my remains.

Various Absences

My Alzheimer's-addled mom picks up
the program for dad's funeral and gasps,

"Dick is dead," as though we, returned
from his rites, might not have heard.

We flip the folded sheet to its other face,
a sepia litho, palm trees and a cross,

beside the church that they attended
these forty years. Reading, she calms,

contemplating the image like a card
dealt her at bridge, thinking of the play

of tricks, until, reversing it to dad's life
summary, she cries again "Dick is dead."

Taking knowledge from her hands,
we unfix memory, lead her back from hell.

Close Call

The Big Bang-like blast of expanding gases made the window shudder. Ten feet away, an unlucky azalea gave up a wisp of sooty material after meeting with one of the bolts that fell daily in Lightning Alley. Too close to that charred hot spot, too close to the conducting glass, I might have shared the sort of connection to the clouds that took up a few souls every summer like the thunderstorms that sucked up frogs and fish from the impoundment ponds. Or, the time an arm forked through the open window of my first floor rental in the Quaker Cooperative presaging a break and enter visitor at two in the morning who would have surely taken up a blocking position between me and my only exit. I was culpable. Neighborly gossip called me out for leaving my window cracked at the same level every night. Gave him the idea no one was home, they said, but I had never expected my formidable padlock could be picked so easily. I shouted, he ran. No one was hurt in the making of this anecdote. That time when I got a burst of chlorine in the face, that time when the lake mud sucked me down to the waist, that time when I heard a dry rattle beside my high-tops in Tennessee: just a few fun facts. Not really near-death experiences; more like near-near-death experiences, all of them unexpected, occurring when everything was quiet, ordinary, domestic. Not like I was stopping for drinks at a biker bar. Not like I was dancing on the edge of a drop-off, or dating a Mafia princess. Not like I was doing something spectacular enough that my end would be called tragic. I just looked around and Bam, another chance encounter. Until then, I hadn't realized that I who moved so deliberately was only an accident waiting to happen.

Obit

Seeing in *The New York Times*
that Kinsella's bought it,
I think to summon up
his poems on the internet,
but find "Mirror in February"
co-opted by pop-ups for Disney
princesses and Quaker Oats,
perhaps, the sort of images
that his line, "idling on some
compulsive fantasy" presaged.

The framing ads are compelling:
sleek ships playing on sparkling
seas, cereals distributing health
to merry families. This is
what we're here for in America.
So much skill goes into making
everyday things look better
that the blandishments of the screen
are more intriguing than the musings
of some poet reflecting on his age.

Kinsella's words went with him,
repatriated, as we all will be.
Swiping left on introspection,
our electronic reflections offer
the therapy of touched-up pictures.
Bad thoughts won't make you a star.
Absent the sag of history at the eyes,
we can live as our own best selfie.
The magic mirror in the cell phone
says, "You are a pretty one. Yes, you are."

The Future

arrives earlier every day
so I try to stay young by using a good moisturizer.
Gravitons can really do a number on your skin.

I can't identify what's changed.
Everyone keeps making it new.
Eternity is boring that way.

If I could exceed light speed I could go back and evolve
into something not recognizable as me.
I'd still be here for you but different.

I mentioned you in my Captain's Log yesterday,
or maybe I didn't.
Circling this black hole words get erased.

Foster's Rule

Foster's rule, also known as the island rule or the island effect, is an ecogeographical rule in evolutionary biology stating that members of a species get smaller or bigger depending on the resources available in the environment. Wikipedia, the free encyclopedia

You have to scale down
to survive when you're confined.
Forget what you were.

Find yourself a size
that's more fit for concealment.
Stay cute as a pet.

Being discounted
is how you go unnoticed
by the predators,

those minor species,
that, unrestrained, grew monstrous:
doctors and nurses.

Where to Put Death

It is always good to put something about dying in the last line of your poem because that gives the reader a start a pause a hmm and maybe even compels him or her to go back and re-read the text that he or she might have just skimmed when they read it the first time because maybe your poem is made up of descriptive language which face it sounds rather plain because maybe your own life is a just a little on the dull side am I right but now your readers can see just what you were really leading up to and that you had a theme so he or she can better grasp the craft you've shown by getting everyone to follow your sly narrative argument which before seemed to involve only some sort of description of the objects in your house or perhaps the workplace but which now they know was riffing on something really big anyway it's always better to throw death in at the end because putting it at the beginning of your poem means it's just another goddam poem about death and that sort of a thing is a buzzkill to most people so save it up for the big finale the big blow off because that's just what life always does I mean like it just did to so many I can't count.

Clearing Things Out

The shallow growing grass is easiest to dislodge.
Harder to pull are the mobs of dominating weeds
that weave through the crumbling loam. I stoop
above the thrust of irises that I would preserve
as I search like Scylla for bodies to rip from the bed,
snatching up worthless oxalis and dandelion,
plantain and purslane, their stubborn clumps
slackening when I shake the soil from their roots.
I exile them from the places that they've seized,
tossing their remains onto the gravel paths to shrivel
under the ruthless sun, though I choose to spare
the sweet violets. Their beauty has calmed my rage
on many wild mornings. In deciding what
I murder, I recognize distinctions, as gods do not.

Double-zero

Birth is the start
of an incredible
lucky streak.

Each breath
is a longshot bet
that pays off.

You watch
as your years
stack up like chips.

Sometimes,
you forget how much
you've won.

Then, the silver ball
falls into
the wrong slot

and the croupier
sweeps his stick
across the felt table.

The house always wins.
You remember that
as you depart.

Sadly

Discussing the passing of a celebrity, the anchorperson throws in a "tragically," as a code word for the general notion that this celebrity died too young although celebrities who have lived long enough to be forgotten get tagged with a "sadly," as in "Sadly, the former celebrity was found dead in his mansion." This can make for a fun party game with everyone guessing the modifier to be applied to the next fatality. Taylor Swift, say, would probably earn a "tragically," while Chubby Checker might get a "sadly." You could even take it to a metaphysical level, debating if the obit should say that "Tragically, God is dead, or whether "sadly" is what suffices. As for yourself, don't worry about whether you will go "sadly" or "tragically." Your passing won't rise to that level of adverbs.

Arrangement

Cut from the stalks that had raised
their brightness to height,
the flowers left the community,

but perked up in the afterlife
of a deco vase, revived and glowing,
made the memory piece of the family.

But their placement was for short display.
Too soon, they were ugly, the color
gone from their faces, flimsy arms drooping.

When they awoke to old age,
their wide brown eyes wept yellow
pollen tears across the dining table.

Their water had a stink to it.
We had loved them; now, they scared us.

Barely There

We let the guard know
one crypt was open. He laughed,
"Sometimes they get out."
That was the last time we took
the short cut through the graveyard.

In Lieu of Flowers

Talking funerals,
how we'd need
to keep the mourners
entertained,

we pondered
what boxed set
best set off
the oblong box.

You wanted
a cranked up
Shane croaking
"Let me go, boys."

For me, Satchmo
singing a gravelly
St. James
Infirmary Blues.

But it was really
our notions
about heaven
we worked through:

what songs
we'd have reverb
through that echo
chamber six feet under.

No headphones
needed, we'd
drift off to what
most pleased us in life:

special requests,
perhaps something
a DJ dropped
around 3:00 am,

grave goods,
lingering, immaterial,
that we might
listen to forever.

La Poesie Me Volera Ma Mort

There was a single
word on my lips
when I expired.

Now, novels
scroll from my corpse.
Pleasure,

you are
the central character
of my fiction.

I direct praise
to you as a tree
sends roots into the soil.

Fixed to earth
I delight
in the purest transmission

of sense.
What I held back,
I make yours, too.

Lungs

Once they seemed as innocent
as a milk bottle soul, these wings

that carried me in updrafts of breath.
Now, they appear on my CT scan

like the peppered moths darkened
by industrial melanism

in Victorian London. Unable
to catch wind, they drag me earthward,

though the longing is still there
to fly invisibly on grafted feathers

like H. C. Andersen's fellow traveler,
that underworld man returned

from his unpaid casket to slay
an ogre and unhex the black swan,

redeeming her beauty,
as these blots, these erasures,

this corruption in the chest,
might yet be the source of creation.

Chris Bullard is a retired judge who lives in Philadelphia, PA. In 2022, Main Street Rag published his poetry chapbook, *Florida Man*, and Moonstone Press published his poetry chapbook, *The Rainclouds of y*. In 2025, his work will appear in *Keystone: Contemporary Poets on Pennsylvania*. He was nominated this year for the Pushcart Prize.

www.ingramcontent.com/pod-product-compliance
Lightning Source LLC
Chambersburg PA
CBHW030053100426
42734CB00038B/1540